Sam Choy's
Little Hawaiian Cookbook
FOR BIG APPETITES

Library of Congress Catalog Card
Number: 2003111838

ISBN-10: 1-56647-647-X
ISBN-13: 978-1-56647-647-8

Eighth Printing, July 2017

Design by Sistenda Yim
All photography by Douglas Peebles

Mutual Publishing, LLC
1215 Center Street, Suite 210
Honolulu, Hawai'i 96816
Ph: (808) 732-1709
Fax: (808) 734-4094
email: info@mutualpublishing.com
www.mutualpublishing.com

Printed in South Korea

INTRODUCTION
▽△▽△▽△▽△▽△▽△▽△▽

Sam Choy's Little Hawaiian Cookbook for Big Appetites is a little taste of the big world of Hawai'i's multicultural cooking. With celebrity chef Sam Choy as your guide, you will find well-loved Island favorites as well as signature dishes that have been skillfully crafted by Chef Choy to show off Hawai'i's bounty and rich cultural heritage.

You can discover the pleasures of poke, Hawai'i's favorite snack food, with three different recipes, **Sam-Style Poke, Korean-Style Tako Poke,** and **Sam Choy's World Famous Fried Marlin Poke.** Sam Choy brought poke into the culinary mainstream through his Annual Sam Choy Poke Festival. You won't want to miss this unique and delicious way to prepare fresh seafood—it may become one of your favorites.

You'll find traditional Hawaiian *lū'au* treats like **Chicken Lū'au** and *Lomi Lomi* **Salmon** to enjoy as well as easy recipes for favorite home-style dishes such as **Quick and Easy Shoyu Chicken.** For special occasions, this book even tells you how to prepare some of Sam's famous restaurant specialties—such as the spectacular **Crusted Ono.**

TABLE OF CONTENTS

Sam-Style Poke

SAM-STYLE POKE

Thousands of entries in the Sam Choy / Aloha Festivals
Poke Recipe Contest and thousands of orders for the many
kinds of poke we serve at the restaurants shows me that
poke is finally going mainstream.

Serves 8

2/3 cup Sam's Secret Sauce *see below
2 pounds finely diced 'ahi (yellowfin tuna)
4 teaspoons 'inamona *see Note below
1 cup rinsed and chopped ogo (seaweed)
1 tablespoon sesame oil
1 teaspoon soy sauce

Combine 'ahi with 'inamona, ogo, sesame oil, and soy sauce. Mix
thoroughly. Add Sam's secret sauce and marinate for 30 to 60
minutes in the refrigerator. Enjoy.

Sam's Secret Sauce

2 cups water
2 tablespoons Hawaiian salt
2 Hawaiian chili peppers, finely chopped

Combine ingredients and stir until salt completely dissolves.

'Inamona *is crushed and roasted* kukui *nuts, usually salted. In
place of* 'inamona *you can substitute 6 teaspoons of crushed,
roasted and salted cashew nuts for a similar taste.*

Calamari Taro Cakes

CALAMARI TARO CAKES

I like going out in the ocean late at night and seeing all the calamari swimming around the lights. They are so easy to catch. Just throw in a glow-stick attached to a hook and all of a sudden you've got a bunch of calamari. If you've never tasted calamari, you ought to give it a try. A member of the squid family, it has a mild flavor, a nice firm texture, and is very economical.

Serves 6

> 2 lbs. calamari tentacles, enough water to cover, enough salt to make water salty
> 1-1/2 cups boiled sweet potatoes, mashed
> 1/2 cups taro, steamed and mashed
> salt and pepper to taste
> 1 teaspoon Chinese parsley, minced
> 1 tablespoon melted butter
> 2 eggs
> 6 slices bacon, finely chopped
> 2 tablespoons flour, or more, as needed
> 1/2 cup clarified butter
> 1/2 cup olive oil

Bring salted water to a boil, drop in tentacles and cook for about 1 minute. Rinse in cold water. Chop coarsely and blend well with sweet potatoes, taro, salt and pepper, Chinese parsley, melted butter, and eggs. Brown bacon and fold into mixture. Divide into 12 equal portions, roll into balls, and flatten into cakes. Dust with flour and fry until golden brown in clarified butter and olive oil. The cakes can also be deep-fried (at 350° to 375°) after being dipped into beaten eggs, then bread crumbs.

Chicken Long Rice

CHICKEN LONG RICE

Long rice is an acquired taste. But once you savor this dish with its chicken and shredded vegetables, and taste how good it is with fresh *poi*, green onions and Hawaiian salt, you'll see why this dish is served at every lū'au.

Serves 12

4 ounces long rice
20 dried shiitake mushrooms
4 cups chicken broth
2 pounds skinless, boneless chicken, cubed
2-inch finger of fresh ginger, crushed
1 medium onion, minced
2 cups thinly sliced celery
2 carrots, julienned
6 green onions, cut in 1-inch lengths

Soak long rice in warm water for 1 hour. Soak mushrooms in warm water for 20 minutes and drain. Remove stems and slice caps. Pour chicken broth into a large pot, add chicken and ginger, and simmer for 5 minutes. Add onion, celery, carrots, and mushrooms, and simmer another 4 to 5 minutes. Drain long rice and cut into 3-inch lengths. Add long rice and green onions to the pot and stir. Cook an additional 5 minutes or until long rice becomes translucent.

CHICKEN *LŪʻAU*

My mom taught me how to do this. Every year we have a big Hawaiian *lūʻau* and the chicken *lūʻau* has to be done the Choy family way.

Makes 8 (1/2-cup) Side-Dish Servings

1 pound *lūʻau* (young taro leaves)
   *see note below
3 cups water
1 tablespoon Hawaiian sea salt
1/2 teaspoon baking soda
3/4 pound skinless, boneless
   chicken breast, cubed
2 tablespoons butter
1/2 medium onion, chopped
1 cup chicken stock
1 cup coconut milk
1/2 teaspoon salt

Rinse *lūʻau* and trim off stems and thick veins. In a stockpot, bring water, Hawaiian salt, and baking soda to a boil. Add *lūʻau* and cook partially covered for 1 hour. Drain off and squeeze out excess liquid. In a large saucepan, heat butter and sauté onions until translucent. Add chicken and cook 3 minutes, stirring frequently. Add chicken stock, coconut milk, cooked *lūʻau*, and salt. Simmer 20 minutes or until chicken is cooked.

Taro, Ancient Mainstay of Hawaiʻi—Taro came by canoe with the earliest Polynesian settlers and has been cultivated as the primary food of the Hawaiian people since ancient times. All parts of this versatile plant are eaten. The leaves, called *lū'au*, are cooked as greens and have a flavor similar to spinach. These greens are very nutritious, supplying high amounts of vitamins A, B, and C, as well as calcium, iron, phosphorus, thiamine, and riboflavin.

Though they contain fewer vitamins, the corms that are made into *poi* are an excellent high-fiber source of carbohydrates. Even the leaf stems, called *hāhā*, are consumed. All parts of the taro plant must be cooked in order to break down the needle-like oxalic acid crystals that can be quite painful if ingested.

There are nearly 200 varieties of taro—the most popular being the *Lehua* variety that has reddish leaves and purple corms. This variety is preferred for making *poi*. The *Pololu* variety is popular for its *lū'au* leaves, and the *'Āpi'i*, a white variety, is favored for making *kūlolo*, a pudding-like confection of grated taro and coconut milk.

Be sure to cook lū'au *(young taro leaves) for the amount of time suggested, as the cooking will break down the oxalic acid crystals. Eating properly cooked* lū'au *is perfectly safe, authentic, and delicious, so be sure to try it. However, if you can't find* lū'au, *you can still make this superb dish with fresh spinach. You can add the washed spinach without pre-cooking at the same time you add the chicken stock.*

Crusted Ono

14

CRUSTED *ONO*

Crusted *ono* is one of the bestsellers. It has a kind of repu-
tation, but it works. People love it. It's very good, very good.

Makes 6 Servings

4 *ono* (wahoo) fillets (6 ounces each)*
1/4 cup olive oil
1 teaspoon fresh ginger, minced
1 teaspoon garlic, minced
Salt and pepper to taste
1/2 cup Ritz® Cracker crumbs
1/2 cup butter at room temperature
1/4 cup macadamia nuts, chopped
1 tablespoon fresh herbs, minced
   (combination of basil, dill and hyme)
1 teaspoon paprika
Papaya-Mango Salsa *see next page

Marinate *ono* in mixture of olive oil, ginger, garlic, salt and pepper.
Preheat oven to 375°. Combine cracker-crumbs, butter, macadamia
nuts, herbs, and paprika; blend well. Divide cracker-crumb mixture
into 4 portions and pat 1 portion on top of each fillet. Bake 8 to 10
minutes. Serve with Papaya-Mango Salsa.

*If ono *cannot be obtained, substitute an equal portion of any firm white-
fleshed fish.*

PAPAYA-MANGO SALSA

Makes 2-1/2 Cups

3 tablespoons sugar
1-1/2 tablespoons vinegar
Pinch red chili pepper flakes
Pinch cumin
1 medium papaya, seeded, peeled, and
  diced
1 cup mango, peeled and diced
1/2 small red onion, diced
3 tablespoons red bell pepper, diced
2 tablespoons cilantro, chopped

Mix sugar, vinegar, chili flakes, and cumin until sugar dissolves.
Fold in remaining ingredients.

This fresh and fruity salsa may also be used as a relish for the Hawaiian Pūlehu Tri-Tip Steak (see p.27) or your favorite recipe for broiled chicken or fish.

BOK CHOY BROCCOLI

Serves 6

2 tablespoons cooking oil

1 medium onion, thinly sliced

1 tablespoon fresh ginger root, grated
or minced

2 cloves garlic, crushed

1/2 teaspoon salt

3 cups fresh broccoli florets, sliced

1 lb. bok choy, coarsely chopped

2 tablespoons lemon juice

1-1/2 teaspoons sugar

1 tablespoon soy sauce

Heat oil in wok or skillet on medium-high until it's almost smoking. Add onion, ginger, garlic, and salt. Stir-fry for 2 minutes. Add broccoli and bok choy and stir-fry for 1 minute. Add lemon juice, sugar, and soy sauce and stir-fry for 3 minutes, or until crisp-tender.

DA WIFE'S BEAN SOUP

At family gatherings, it's the wife's soup or mine. My soup always has leftovers, her soup's always gone. (I think we eat more to make her feel better — just kidding!)

Makes 18 Servings

2 cups dried beans (kidney, pinto, or small red)

2 smoked ham hocks or ham shanks

3 cups chicken stock

1 cup chopped cilantro

2 cups diced potatoes

2 cups diced carrots

1-1/2 cups diced onion

1/2 cup diced celery

1 Portuguese sausage (10 ounces)

2 cups tomato purée

Salt and pepper to taste

Soak beans in water overnight. Drain. In a stockpot, combine soaked beans, ham hocks, chicken stock, cilantro, and water to cover (about 6 cups). Bring to a boil, then simmer until meat and beans are tender. Remove skin and bones from ham hocks; shred meat and return to stock. Slice and fry Portuguese sausage, and blot with paper towel. Add sausage to stockpot along with potatoes, carrots, onion, celery and tomato purée. Cook until potatoes are tender. Season with salt and pepper. Goes great with fresh baked bread.

A Taste of Portugal—This recipe is a variation of Portuguese Bean Soup, a prized dish that has become a part of Hawai'i's local cuisine. The Portuguese, mostly from the Azores and Madeira, started arriving in Hawai'i in 1878, adding to her vibrant ethnic mix of people. Delicious Portuguese sausage, a spicy and garlicky favorite to be eaten for breakfast or as an ingredient in many dishes, is one of the many culinary gifts from the Portuguese to the Hawaiian table.

Portuguese sweet bread, a light and tender round loaf that is sold in every Hawai'i supermarket, is a popular accompaniment to this soup.

Da Wife's Bean Soup

GINGER *ONO*

Coming from a fishing village on the North Shore of O'ahu, I grew up catching and eating fish as a way of life and learned early which fish were good for cooking, which for eating raw, and which for making traditional Hawaiian poke. I started playing around with preparing fish in different ways, and one of the combinations I really liked was ono sashimi with ginger sauce. People rave about how good it is. They can't believe it's ono.

Serves 6

1 pound fresh raw *ono*

1-1/2 cups assorted sprouts

1/2 cup Local *Pepe'ekeo* Dip **see below*

Thinly slice raw *ono*. Line small platter or individual plates with sprouts of your choice. Arrange *ono* slices on sprouts. Spoon Local *Pepe'ekeo* Dip over the raw fish and serve chilled. (If you've never tried raw fish, you'll be surprised how good this tastes.)

Local *Pepe'ekeo* Dip

1/2 cup oil

1/2 teaspoon salt

1 clove garlic, minced

1/4 cup ginger, minced

1/4 cup green onions, minced

1/4 cup lightly packed Chinese parsley, minced

1/8 teaspoon white pepper

1/4 teaspoon red pepper flakes, or

1 fresh Hawaiian chili pepper, minced

In a small saucepan heat oil, add salt, and cook for 2 to 3 minutes. Cool. Stir in garlic, ginger, green onions, Chinese parsley, white pepper, and red pepper. Chill. Makes 3/4 cup.

Selecting Fish to be Served Raw—Although it's always a good idea to buy the freshest fish, when you make a raw fish preparation, freshness becomes even more important. Any off flavors or odors are amplified when seafood is eaten raw, so be sure that the fish you select meet these criteria:

1. The fish should not smell "fishy." Though this may sound like a contradiction, a "fishy" odor means the product is too old. The fish should have very little odor—and what odor there is should be clean—almost like cucumber or seaweed.

2. If you're buying filleted or pre-cut fish, the color of the flesh should be bright and clear, without any brownish tones. Avoid pieces with wide bands of gristle or large blood spots.

3. If the fish is pre-packaged, make sure the date on the package is the latest possible.

4. If you're buying the fish whole, the whites of the eyes should be clear and bulging, not cloudy or bloody and sunken. The color of the body should be bright and characteristic of the species, and the scales should be firmly attached. If you lift up one of the gill covers, the inside should be bright red. If you poke the belly area, the part you press should spring back.

GRANDMA'S MEATLOAF

My mom makes a good meatloaf. She said, oh, that's Grandma's meatloaf. My grandparents weren't around when I was growing up, so I just have to listen when my mom tells all the stories.

Meatloaf Mixture

1-1/2 pounds lean ground beef
1/2 pound ground chicken
1-1/2 cups toasted bread crumbs
1 can (8-1/4 ounces) crushed pineapple, drained well
1/2 cup chopped onion
1/2 cup chopped celery
2 eggs
1/4 cup heavy cream or milk
1/4 cup soy sauce
1 tablespoon minced ginger
Salt and black pepper to taste
Chopped green onions
1 cup Tailgate Teri Glaze
*see opposite page

Preheat oven to 350°. Combine meatloaf mixture ingredients, blending lightly but well. Press into a loaf pan. Bake 50 minutes. Pour 1/4 cup Tailgate Teri Glaze over meatloaf 5 minutes before the end of cooking time. Slice meatloaf, sprinkle with green onions and serve with remaining 3/4 cup Tailgate Teri Glaze.

Meatloaf mixture can be formed into meatballs. Bake meatballs at 350° for 25 to 30 minutes, depending on size. Then, simmer meatballs 5 minutes in Tailgate Teri Glaze. These are excellent as a pupu or an entrée.

Tailgate Teri Sauce—Makes 2 Cups

1 cup soy sauce
Juice from 1 medium orange
1/2 cup mirin
1/2 cup water
1/4 cup brown sugar
1-1/2 teaspoons minced garlic
1-1/2 teaspoons minced ginger

Combine all ingredients and blend well.

Garlic Mashed Potatoes— Makes About 6 Cups

2-1/4 pounds potatoes
4 whole cloves garlic
1/2 pound butter
6 tablespoons heavy cream
Salt and white pepper to taste

Fill a pot with 3 inches of cold water. Peel and cut the potatoes into 1-inch cubes and add them to the pot. Add additional cold water to cover potatoes. Add garlic and bring to a boil. Cook for 8 to 10 minutes or until done. Drain. Purée in a food processor, or whip with an electric mixer. Add the butter and cream. Season with salt and white pepper. Serve immediately.

HAWAIIAN PRIME RIB AU JUS

Serves 8 to 10

7-lb. standing rib roast	1 cup celery, chunked
5 garlic cloves, crushed	1 cup onions, chunked
1 tablespoon salt mixed with	16 oz. chicken broth
1/2 tablespoon cracked pepper	16 oz. beef broth
1 tablespoon garlic salt	1/2 cup cornstarch mixed
1 tablespoon rosemary mixed	with 1/4 cup water
with 1/2 teaspoon thyme	salt and pepper to taste
1 cup carrots, chunked	

Preheat oven to 350°. Peel back fat cover and place garlic cloves on meat, then sprinkle with half of salt/cracked pepper/garlic salt mixture. Roll fat cover back into place and sprinkle top of fat with remaining salt mixture and herbs.

Place meat on rack in deep roasting pan and roast for 45 minutes. Add to pan chunked vegetables and broths, making sure rack is high enough so liquid doesn't touch meat (you may have to use less broth).

Continue roasting meat until internal temperature reaches 130°. Let rest about half an hour after removing from oven before slicing.

To make gravy, remove roast from pan and place pan on burner. Skim off fat. Bring drippings to a boil, then add cornstarch/water mixture, stirring constantly, until thickened. Adjust seasonings with salt and pepper, strain, and keep warm.

Carve meat to whatever thickness you like and serve with gravy and all the trimmings.

HULI HULI (ROTISSERIE) BEEF

Serves 10 to 12

> 1 whole cross-rib roast (4 lbs.), or
>   bottom round, or tri-tip
> 4 cups sweet vermouth, for basting

Marinade

> 1 tablespoon cracked peppercorns
> sea salt, as needed, up to 1 cup
> 2 tablespoons garlic, minced
> 2 tablespoons ginger, minced

Combine marinade ingredients, massage into roast, and let marinate 15 minutes. Place roast on skewer and secure into rotisserie over hot coals. (Don't cover.)

Plan on about 2 hours cooking time. Baste every 10 to 20 minutes with sweet vermouth, until the last 30 minutes. Then baste about every 5 minutes. If you don't have a rotisserie, it can be done in a closed outdoor barbecue system by turning the meat every half hour and basting in the same manner as for the rotisserie method.

It's very impressive when you go to a backyard party or a family gathering and see this massive side of beef turning over the coals, and you ask yourself how you can do it at home. That's why I've included this recipe, so you can do rotisserie beef yourself and have it look awesome and impressive, as well as have it taste really good.

Hawaiian Pūlehu *Tri-Tip Steak*

HAWAIIAN *PŪLEHU* TRI-TIP STEAK

Crusty on the outside and rare on the inside. That's the secret to this mouthwatering dish. It could almost be called beef sashimi. Hot is wonderful, but cold sandwiches the next day allow the flavors to mature very nicely, thank you.

Serves 4 to 6

2-1/2 pounds tri-tip steak (triangular tip of the sirloin)

1/2 cup sea salt

1 tablespoon fresh garlic, minced

1/2 tablespoon cracked peppercorns

1 tablespoon granulated sugar

Prepare your charcoal for grilling.

Rub salt, garlic, pepper, and sugar into the meat and let sit 30 minutes. *Pūlehu* in Hawaiian means "to broil on hot embers" and that's what you do, turning the meat every 4 minutes until done. Total cooking time is about 10 to 15 minutes, depending on the thickness of the cut.

ISLAND BRAISED LAMB SHANKS

Serves 6 to 10

        3 lbs. lamb shanks
        1/2 cup vegetable oil
        4 cloves garlic, minced
        8 cups chicken broth or stock (or
            enough to cover meat)
        1/2 teaspoon ground Chinese Five Spice
        1/2 cup Chinese parsley
        5 tablespoons dry sherry
        2 tablespoons brown sugar
        1 finger fresh ginger root, sliced
        5 tablespoons soy sauce
        1/2 cup onions, julienned
        1/2 cup celery, julienned
        1/2 cup red bell pepper, julienned
        1/2 cup yellow bell pepper, julienned
        4 tablespoons cornstarch blended well
            with 3 tablespoons water, for thickening

In a large stockpot brown lamb shanks with garlic in 1/2 cup oil (reserving 4 tablespoons of oil for later use) until golden brown, about 6 to 8 minutes over medium-high heat. Cover meat with chicken broth, then add Chinese Five Spice, Chinese parsley, sherry, brown sugar, ginger, and soy sauce. Bring to a boil on stove top, cover with foil or oven-proof lid and place in 350° oven. Braise for about 1 hour, or until tender.

Remove lamb and strain stock. Set stock and lamb aside and keep warm.

In a large skillet, heat 4 tablespoons oil over medium-high heat and stir-fry onions, celery, and peppers for about 2 to 3 minutes, then add stock and bring to a boil. While it's boiling, add cornstarch mixture and cook until thickened.

Arrange shanks nicely on a platter, and cover with vegetable/sauce mixture.

Home cooks don't usually think much about presentation, but when you arrange food artistically on the plate, it enhances the flavor. Even a TV dinner—if you take it out of the tin and put it on a plate and add a sprig of fresh parsley—it only takes a minute, but it really makes the food seem to taste better. It's like the presentation sets up your taste buds; if your eye sees something that looks good, you're going to enjoy it more. I like using a vertical presentation, which is sort of a "new wave" thing. Who says you have to serve pork chops the boring old traditional way with the mashed potatoes on one side and the vegetable on the other? Why not make eating more exciting and fun by putting the mashed potatoes in the middle of the plate, stir-fried vegetables on top of the potatoes, and the pork chops on top of that, with a colorful garnish to top it all off? The height makes it look elegant, and all the flavors blended together in every bite makes it taste really good.

Korean-Style Tako Poke

KOREAN-STYLE *TAKO* POKE

Ethnic variation: In this poke, Korean garlic-chili sauce offers a really exciting flavor; you could make your own—just grind up garlic and local peppers with salt.

Serves 6

2 pounds fresh *ogo* (edible seaweed)

1 pound *tako* (octopus)

1 Maui onion, diced

1/2 cup chopped green onion

1 cup rice vinegar, available in Asian section of markets

1/2 cup soy sauce

1/2 cup sugar

3 tablespoons roasted sesame seeds

2 tablespoons bottled *Korean kochu jang* (hot chili paste), available in Asian section of supermarkets and in Asian markets

1 teaspoon minced fresh ginger

2 cloves garlic, minced

Cut *ogo* in 2-inch lengths. Cook *tako* and slice. In a mixing bowl, combine all ingredients. Serve very cold at tailgate and backyard barbecues.

New Wave Marinated 'Ahi Salad

NEW WAVE MARINATED *'AHI* SALAD

This delicious salad offers an interesting contrast in tastes and textures between chilled greens, cold noodles, and warm fish. You can make it low-cal by omitting the deep-fried flour tortilla and the oil used in the marinade and using a low-fat dressing.

Serves 1

> 3 *'ahi* fillets (2 oz. each and about 1/2 in. thick)
>
> 1 tablespoon olive oil for searing fish (or enough to coat bottom of pan)
>
> 2–3 oz. Japanese soba noodles, or somen
>
> 1 flour tortilla
>
> salad greens (a handful or two)
>
> salad dressing of your choice

Garnishes

> carrot, beet, and radish curls, or grated carrots and zucchini
>
> 3 cucumber slices
>
> 3 tomato slices
>
> sprig or two of Chinese parsley
>
> sprinkle of black sesame seeds,
>
> chopped macadamia nuts, or chopped walnuts

continued on the next page

Marinade—for one portion, makes about 1 cup

1/2 cup soy sauce
1/4 cup light salad oil
2 tablespoons mirin
1/4 teaspoon sesame oil
1/2 tablespoon Chinese parsley, minced
2 tablespoons green onions, thinly sliced
1 tablespoon garlic, minced
1 tablespoon ginger, minced
1/2 teaspoon salt
1/4 teaspoon white pepper
1-1/2 teaspoons brown sugar
1/2 teaspoon ground Chinese Five Spice
1 tablespoon black sesame seeds
1 pinch dried red pepper flakes, or
1 fresh Hawaiian chili pepper

Combine all marinade ingredients and blend well. Remove 2 tablespoons of marinade (or more, to taste) before marinating fish, and set aside to use later on noodles. Marinate 'ahi fillets in mixture for 5 minutes, or less, then remove fish and set aside.

Cook soba noodles (or somen) according to package directions, rinse well in cold water and drain. Take the 2 tablespoons of marinade you set aside and mix it with noodles. Chill noodles in the fridge for 20 to 30 minutes.

Have everything ready to go before you cook the 'ahi so that the fish will be hot when you serve it. Also wait until the last minute before placing the greens and noodles on the tortilla, or it will become soggy.

Papa Choy's Beef Tomato

PAPA CHOY'S BEEF TOMATO

My dad taught me this one when I was about 14. When I used to come home from school as a kid, my dad would go to the refrigerator and bring out all these vegetables and wash and chop and slice them and lay them out in a pan, then take some beef and slice it thin and marinate it, then stir-fry it all together and within minutes I'd be sitting there eating it. It's just amazing how quick he could do it, and how good it tasted.

Serves 6

1 lb. round steak, flank steak, or beef of your choice

1 tablespoon oil

3 medium fresh tomatoes, cut into wedges

1 medium onion, sliced into half moons

1 large green pepper, sliced into strips

4 stalks green onions, cut into 1-in. lengths

2 stalks celery, thinly sliced on the diagonal

Salt and pepper to taste

Marinade

1 tablespoon soy sauce

1 tablespoon sherry

1 tablespoon oil

1-1/2 teaspoons sugar

continued on the next page

                    1 clove garlic, minced
                    1/4 finger fresh ginger, sliced
Sauce
                    1 cup chicken broth
                    1 tablespoon cornstarch
                    2 tablespoons soy sauce
                    2 teaspoons salt
                    2 teaspoons brown sugar
                    1 teaspoon oyster sauce

Slice beef thinly into strips, or bite-sized pieces. Combine marinade ingredients, mix well and massage into meat. Let marinate for 30 minutes. Combine sauce ingredients, mix well, and set aside.

Heat 1 tablespoon oil in a wok or frying pan on medium-high. Stir-fry beef about 2 minutes, remove beef from pan and set aside. Add vegetables to pan and stir-fry until onions are translucent, about 3 minutes. Add sauce to vegetables. Cook about 2 minutes, until it comes to a boil. Add beef and adjust seasonings with salt and pepper. Serve over hot rice.

POKE PATTIES

This is like tartare, except we cut the fish in tiny cubes and make a patty similar to a hamburger. We sear it, yet on the inside it's rare, with poke-style seasoning.

Makes 2 Patties

Panko (packaged Japanese-style fine breadcrumbs) or
   Italian breadcrumbs

2 tablespoons canola oil

Patties

1 cup diced very fresh 'ahi (yellowfin tuna) or aku
   (skipjack tuna), cut in about 1/4- to 3/8-inch cubes

1/4 cup minced onion

1/4 cup minced green onions

1 egg

2 tablespoons chopped fresh ogo (edible seaweed)

2 tablespoons soy sauce   1 teaspoon sesame oil

Pinch EACH salt, pepper

Sauce

1/4 cup sliced mushrooms	1 teaspoon oyster sauce
2 tablespoons butter	1 teaspoon chopped
1 teaspoon soy sauce	cilantro

Combine patty ingredients and form 2 patties. Press patties in panko to coat. In a frying pan, heat oil over medium-high heat. Gently place patties in pan and brown both sides, keeping the inside of patties medium rare.

To make sauce, sauté mushrooms in butter 2 minutes. Add remaining sauce ingredients and cook 1 minute. Pour sauce over patties and serve as pupu, or appetizers.

BEEF NOODLE SALAD WITH PEANUTS

Makes 6 Cups

1 pound beef round tip	3 tablespoons soy sauce
6-1/2 ounces dry cellophane noodles	2 tablespoons sweet chili sauce
1 tablespoon chili oil	1/4 cup fresh chopped cilantro leaves
1 teaspoon peeled and chopped garlic	1/3 cup roughly chopped, roasted unsalted peanuts
1 cup shredded snow peas	1 lime, cut into 6 wedges
1 tablespoon seeded and sliced hot red peppers	

Slice beef into strips, first cutting across the grain and then with the grain.

Place cellophane noodles in a medium-size bowl and cover with boiling water. Allow to stand for 4 minutes or until soft; drain. Set aside.

Heat wok to high. Add chili oil and garlic and stir for 30 seconds. Add beef and stir-fry for 3 minutes or until seared. Add snow peas and hot peppers and stir-fry for 2 minutes.

Mix soy sauce and sweet chili together and add to beef mixture. Stir briefly and remove from heat.

Toss stir-fry with cellophane noodles, cilantro leaves, and chopped peanuts. Place on a serving platter and serve with wedges of lime.

Taste as you add in the chili, peppers, garlic, and cilantro. Make it a full flavor, not full of fire.

QUICK AND EASY SHOYU CHICKEN

Shoyu (Soy Sauce) chicken, an island classic, features gourmet touches of cilantro, Chinese five spices, and fresh-squeezed orange juice.

Serves 6

1 tablespoon minced cilantro
1/2 teaspoon Chinese Five Spice powder, available in supermarkets
2 pounds chicken thighs
1 tablespoon cornstarch
2 tablespoons water
Green onions
Bean sprouts
Tailgate Teri Sauce *see page 21*

In a medium saucepan, combine Tailgate Teri Sauce, cilantro, and Chinese Five Spice powder. Bring to a boil, add chicken, then simmer 20 minutes or until tender. Remove chicken from sauce, set aside, and keep warm.

Blend cornstarch and water to make a smooth paste. Bring 1 cup of sauce to a boil and stir in cornstarch paste to thicken into a glaze. Brush chicken with glaze. Garnish with green onions and bean sprouts.

TRADITIONAL LOMI LOMI SALMON

Here in Hawai'i the *lū'au* is the traditional way of celebrating a special occasion. They are held for birthdays, anniversaries, weddings, grand openings of new businesses, blessings of boats, the opening or closing of a special event, and for any other reason somebody feels like celebrating. And we're not talking *pupu* or crackers and cheese—this is heavy eating, true feasting. It's a tradition in Hawai'i to hold a baby *lū'au* on your child's first birthday, as a way of giving thanks that your baby made it through the first year, because in the old days lots of babies didn't make it to their first birthday. Anywhere from 50 to 5,000 people will show up for one of these baby *lū'au*, and it's real festive, with Hawaiian entertainment and endless food, and it can go on for two or three days.

Serves 12

> 2 cups salted salmon, diced
> 6 tomatoes, diced
> 2 small red onions, diced
> 1/2 cup green onion, thinly sliced
> 1 Hawaiian chili pepper, or
> 1/8 teaspoon red pepper flakes (optional)

Combine all ingredients and mix well. Serve well chilled. (Salted salmon comes with various degrees of saltiness, so it's a good idea to taste it before making this dish. If it's too salty, you need to soak it overnight in enough water to cover, and then rinse it twice before using.)

SAM CHOY'S WORLD-FAMOUS FRIED MARLIN POKE

Serve 1,000 pounds of this dish in my Kona restaurant each week, and I'm not kidding when I say it's world famous!

Serves 6

4 to 6 ounces of raw marlin cut into 3/4-inch cubes

Sauce

1 teaspoon soy sauce
1/4 cup chopped round onion
1 teaspoon green onion
1/4 cup *ogo* seaweed
1 teaspoon sesame oil
1 tablespoon hot oil
Bean sprouts
Cabbage

For each serving, take 4 to 6 ounces of raw marlin (no other fish works as well as marlin in this recipe), and cut into 3/4-inch cubes. Place cubes in a mixing bowl with 1 teaspoon soy sauce, 1/4 cup chopped round onion, 1 teaspoon green onion, 1/4 cup *ogo* seaweed, and 1 teaspoon sesame oil. Mix well, then quickly sear in 1 tablespoon hot oil (or enough to cover bottom of pan) on high heat in a wok. Don't cook for more than a minute or two, as you want the center raw. Serve on a bed of bean sprouts, chopped cabbage, or greens.

When I cook fish I do it Chinese-style, by quickly searing it on high heat to seal in flavor and moisture; it's one of the secrets that makes the fish I serve at my restaurants taste so good. You have to be careful when using this technique, though, because if you don't remove the fish quickly from the hot pan it will over-cook. Basically, you just slap the fish in the pan, sizzle it on all sides, and remove. You need to add enough oil to coat the bottom of your wok or skillet so the fish won't stick, and heat the oil until it's almost smoking before you add the fish.

Sam Choy's World-Famous Fried Marlin Poke

STEAMED *MAHIMAHI LAULAU*

Serves 4

> 2 cups carrots, finely julienned
> 2 cups zucchini, finely julienned
> 1 cup shiitake mushrooms, sliced
> 8 ti leaves
> 12 fresh *mahimahi* fillets (2 oz. each)
>   (don't substitute any other fish)
> Salt and pepper to taste
> Enough string to tie each *laulau*

Herb sauce

> 1-1/2 cups mayonnaise
> 1 tablespoon soy sauce
> 1 tablespoon fresh dill, chopped

Mix carrots and zucchini together and divide into 4 equal portions. Divide mushrooms into 4 equal portions. Mix herb sauce ingredients and set aside. Remove hard rib from ti leaves to make flexible, or cook leaves on high in microwave for 1 minute to soften.

To build each *laulau*, first make a ti leaf cross on the table by laying 1 ti leaf over another at right angles. Sprinkle vegetable-mix in the center, then lay a *mahimahi* fillet on top of the vegetables. Spread a thin layer of herb sauce on fish and sprinkle with more vegetables. Place another fillet on top, spread with herb sauce, sprinkle with vegetables. Finish with a third fillet that is topped with herb sauce, vegetable mix, and a sprinkle of mushrooms. Season with salt and pepper to taste.

Gather up ti leaves to make a purse around fish and tie tightly with string just above bundle. Repeat for all four portions, using a fourth of the vegetables, a fourth of the mushrooms, and three *mahimahi* fillets for each *laulau*. Steam for 8 to 10 minutes.

Even though the ti leaf wrapper of a laulau isn't eaten, it adds its own unique scent to the dish. For this reason, ti leaves are used throughout Polynesia as a wrap for foods of many kinds. It is worth making the effort to use ti leaves, but if you can't obtain them, you can use parchment paper instead. Make bundles by tying the loose edges of paper above the ingredients in a topknot.

Steamed Mahimahi Laulau

Summer 'Ahi Tartare

46

SUMMER *'AHI* TARTARE

> When you clean just-caught *'ahi*, the bones always have a lot of meat. Get a big spoon, scoop it out, chop that up and make a fine poke, like tartare—the best.

Makes 6 Servings

1 pound very fresh *'ahi* (yellowfin tuna)
1/4 cup minced Maui onion
Juice of 1 lemon
2 tablespoons chopped cilantro
1 tablespoon minced fresh ginger
1 tablespoon soy sauce
1 teaspoon olive oil
1 teaspoon sesame seed oil
1-1/2 teaspoons grated fresh horseradish
1/2 teaspoon prepared stone-ground mustard
Pinch red chili pepper flakes
Salt and white pepper to taste

Cut *'ahi* into 1-inch cubes.

In a food processor, combine all ingredients and pulsate 6 times or until of desired texture; do not purée mixture. If you don't have a processor, mince *'ahi* with a knife to a uniformly coarse texture before combining with other ingredients.

Serve with toast points or crackers and *shiso* (beefsteak plant) leaves.

TRADITIONAL BACKYARD BEEF TERIYAKI

One of the really nice things about living in Hawai'i is being able to barbecue all year long. When anybody in the neighborhood puts something on the grill, that aroma makes your taste buds go wildly out of control and you know that first chance you get you gotta make barbecue yourself. Teriyaki is one of those things everybody does, but it's a real winner. You can't go wrong with it.

Serves 4 to 6

> 2 lbs. thinly sliced steak of your choice

Marinade

> 3 cups soy sauce
> 2 cups sugar
> 1/2 cup ginger, minced
> 4 cloves garlic, minced
> 4 tablespoons green onions, thinly sliced
> 1/4 teaspoon white pepper
> 2 tablespoons Chinese parsley
> 2 teaspoons sesame oil

Blend marinade ingredients well, and marinate meat 4 to 6 hours in the fridge.

Grill over hot coals (a hibachi seems to make the best flavor) for 2 to 3 minutes on each side, or to desired doneness. The meat is thin, so you don't want to overcook it. After it's done, try drizzling on a little of my Special Teriyaki Glaze.

Special Teriyaki Glaze

1/2 cup soy sauce
1/4 cup *mirin*
1/4 cup water
2 tablespoons brown sugar
1 teaspoon garlic, minced
1 teaspoon ginger, minced
1 tablespoon cornstarch mixed with
2 tablespoons water

In a small saucepan bring all ingredients, except cornstarch mixture, to a boil. Blend cornstarch and water to make a smooth paste. Stir into pan. Reduce heat and simmer, stirring frequently, until thickened.

THE BEST BEEF STEW

Makes 6 Servings

4 lbs. chuck roast, cut up
1/2 cup salad oil
2 cloves garlic, crushed
1 small onion, minced
1/2 cup celery leaves
5 cups beef stock, or broth
2 cups chicken broth
1-1/2 cups tomato paste
3 medium carrots, chunked
4 potatoes, chunked
2 medium onions, chunked
4 stalks celery, chunked
Enough flour to dust meat (about 1 cup)
Salt and pepper to taste
Enough *mochiko* and water to thicken

Sprinkle beef with salt and pepper, then dust with flour. Brown meat with garlic, minced onion, and celery leaves about 10 minutes on medium or low-medium, until well browned. Keep stirring to avoid burning.

Drain oil. Add beef and chicken broth and tomato paste. Bring to a boil, then reduce to simmer. Cover and let cook about 1 hour, or until beef is tender.

Add carrots and potatoes and cook 5 minutes. Add onion chunks and celery and cook 10 minutes more. Adjust seasonings with salt and pepper.

One of my secrets for making a thick, rich stew is that I use *mochiko* (sweet rice flour) mixed with a little water for thickening. Bring stew to a boil, add sweet rice flour/water mixture a little at a time, simmering and stirring until you get the right consistency. This stew is best the next day, after all the flavors have had a chance to blend.

I think the thing that makes this recipe so good is the simplicity of it, and the fact that very little seasoning is used, letting the natural flavors of the food shine through.

The Best Beef Stew

ORIENTAL MACADAMIA NUT CHICKEN SALAD WITH FRIED NOODLES

Serves 4

- 4 boneless chicken breasts (8 oz. each)
- 2 tablespoons oil; enough oil for deep-fat frying
- 1-oz. package rice noodles
- 12 wonton wrappers, cut into strips and deep-fried
- 1 medium head iceburg lettuce, shredded
- 10 Chinese parsley sprigs, coarsely chopped
- 2 cups napa cabbage or wonbok, finely chopped
- 1 cup bean sprouts
- 1 cup red bell pepper, julienned
- 1 cup yellow bell pepper, julienned
- 1/2 cup green onions, thinly sliced (diagonally)
- 1 medium carrot, grated
- 6 radishes, thinly sliced
- 1 cup whole macadamia nuts
- 4 whole Chinese parsley sprigs, for garnish
- 1 head leaf lettuce, divided into leaves, for salad bed

Marinade for Chicken

1 cup soy sauce
1 cup oil
4 tablespoons *mirin*
1 teaspoon sesame oil
4 tablespoons Chinese parsley, minced
2 tablespoons garlic, minced
2 tablespoons ginger, minced
1 teaspoon salt
1/2 teaspoon white pepper
2 tablespoons green onions, thinly sliced
4 tablespoons cornstarch
3 teaspoons brown sugar

Combine and blend all marinade ingredients, except for cornstarch and brown sugar, which you will first mix together then add to marinade ingredients. Add chicken and marinate for 1 to 2 hours in the fridge.

Heat oil to 350°. Drop rice noodles in oil and remove as soon as they puff up. (Don't brown them.) Drain on paper towels and break into bite-sized pieces when cool. Set aside.

Cut wonton wrappers into strips and deep-fry until golden brown in same oil you used for rice noodles. Drain on paper towels and set aside.

As soon as everything else is done and iceberg lettuce and other vegetables are sliced, chopped, and refrigerated, you can cook the chicken. Fry in 2 tablespoons oil, with skin on, until golden brown. Start on high heat, then finish on medium. After you turn the heat down, you can baste chicken with marinade.

continued on the next page

Continue basting, using about 1/2 cup of marinade in all, until liquid is absorbed and chicken is nicely browned. When done, let cool to room temperature and cut into strips.

Toss lettuce, cabbage, bean sprouts, and vegetables together with chicken and bite-sized pieces of rice noodles in mixing bowl. Add half of macadamia nuts and half of fried wonton strips, and toss with salad, reserving remaining nuts and won ton strips for garnish.

Arrange on individual salad plates on a bed of your favorite leaf lettuce. Use 1/4 of remaining macadamia nuts, 1/4 of remaining fried won ton strips, and a sprig of Chinese parsley to garnish each salad.

Serve with your choice of dressing. I especially like the Sweet and Sour Cucumber Vinaigrette with this particular salad.

> *Take a piece of chicken, marinate it, cover it with macadamia nuts, deep-fat fry it, or pan fry it, and serve it with fried noodles on mixed salad greens and one of our signature dressings, and you have yourself a surprisingly elegant, simple-to-prepare, and very satisfying salad.*

WASABI VINAIGRETTE

Certain salads need spicing up to reach their peak. Wasabi adds a whole different flavor. I knew it was really popular with sushi and sashimi, so I wanted to play with it in a vinaigrette where people would notice it and have it wake up their taste buds, but where it wouldn't be overpowering.

Makes 3 Cups

2 cups freshly squeezed orange juice	1/2 cup oil
	3 tablespoons vinegar
2 tablespoons sesame seeds	2 tablespoons soy sauce
	Salt to taste
3 tablespoons sugar	2 tablespoons wasabi

Mix all ingredients together and blend well.

CREAMY ORIENTAL DRESSING

This is one of our own inventions and a real hit at our restaurant. I want to share it, because I always enjoy sharing a good thing—it makes me feel good. It's a very simple recipe, using some basic ingredients that you wouldn't normally think of putting together. It goes really well with all our marinated-fish salads, adding another layer of interesting flavors.

Makes 3 Cups

3 cups mayonnaise	1/4 teaspoon white pepper
1/2 cup soy sauce	1-1/2 tablespoons black sesame seeds
3/4 cup sugar	
	1 tablespoon sesame oil

Whisk all ingredients together until well blended. If it's too thick you can whisk in a little water, a few drops at a time, until you get the consistency you like.

(left) You Are the Bestest
(right) Sam's North Shore Smoothie

YOU ARE THE BESTEST

1 ounce Kahlua®
1 ounce Bailey's Irish Cream®
1 ounce coconut syrup
1 ounce ripe banana
1 ounce half & half cream
Ice

Garnish

1 slice of banana
1/4 slice of pineapple

Fill blender with ice to 1/3 full. Add ingredients and blend until creamy. Pour mixture into Reidel® glass, and garnish with a slice of banana and 1/4 slice of a pineapple.

SAM'S NORTH SHORE SMOOTHIE

1 ounce vodka
1 ounce orange juice
1 ounce cranberry juice
2 ounces strawberry purée
1 ounce grenadine syrup
Ice

Garnish

1 slice of banana
1/4 slice of pineapple

Fill blender with ice to 1/3 full. Add ingredients, and blend. Pour mixture into a Viva Grande® glass, and top with whipped cream. Garnish with a maraschino cherry.

PINEAPPLE *HAUPIA*

Serves 12

> 6 cups canned or fresh coconut milk
> 1 cup cornstarch
> 1 cup sugar
> 1/2 teaspoon salt
> 1 cup crushed pineapple

Drain pineapple, squeeze out excess liquid and set aside. Combine coconut milk, cornstarch, sugar, and salt. Stir until cornstarch is dissolved. Cook on medium heat, stirring constantly, until it reaches the boiling point, then reduce to low. When it begins to thicken, add the pineapple and mix well. Pour into individual dessert bowls, or sorbet glasses, and serve either warm or cold, topped with whipped cream. To serve cold, chill for at least 1 hour.

MACADAMIA NUT PIE

Serves 8

> 3 eggs
> 2/3 cup granulated sugar
> 1 cup light corn syrup
> 1-1/2 to 2 cups chopped macadamia nuts
> 2 tablespoons melted butter
> 1 teaspoon vanilla
> 1 unbaked 9-inch pie shell

Preheat oven to 325°. Beat eggs with sugar and corn syrup and stir in the macadamia nuts. Add butter and vanilla and blend well. Pour mixture into pie shell. Bake for 50 minutes or until the crust is golden and the center is somewhat set. Test this by shaking the pie gently. Let cool and chill.

LILIKO'I CHIFFON CREAM PIE

▰▱▰▱▰▱▰▱▰▱▰▱▰▱▰▱▰▱▰▱▰

Fresh *liliko'i* juice is a must for this recipe. That makes it only more 'onolicious, since the *liliko'i* season isn't long. The fluffy egg whites keep it light; the whipped cream makes it almost sinful. Enjoy!

Serves 8

1 tablespoon unflavored gelatin

1/4 cup cold water

4 eggs, separated

1 cup granulated sugar

1/2 teaspoon salt

1/2 cup fresh *liliko'i* juice* (passion fruit)

1 teaspoon grated lemon rind

1 9-inch baked pie shell

1/2 cup cream, whipped

Enough toasted shredded coconut to sprinkle on top

Soften the gelatin in the water. Beat in the egg yolk until thick and add 1/2 cup of the sugar, the salt, and the *liliko'i* juice. Mix well. Over a low heat, stir until the mixture is thickened, about 10 minutes. Add gelatin mixture and stir until the gelatin is dissolved. Remove from heat. Add lemon rind and cool until slightly congealed. Beat egg whites with remaining 1/2 cup of sugar until stiff. Fold into gelatin mixture and pour into a cooled, baked pie shell and chill until firm. Top with whipped cream and sprinkles of toasted coconut.

This recipe requires fresh yellow liliko'i juice.

MANGO BREAD

I like mango bread. Here in the Islands, it's a tradition to make it and give it away. You can make French toast with it. You can toast it... it's fun sitting around peeling mangoes.

Makes 2 Loaves, or 24 Slices

2 cups flour
2 teaspoons baking soda
1 teaspoon baking powder
2 teaspoons cinnamon
3 eggs, well beaten
3/4 cup canola oil
1-1/2 cups sugar
2 cups peeled and diced fresh mango*
1/2 cup raisins
1/2 cup chopped macadamia nuts or
    walnuts
1/2 cup grated coconut

Preheat oven to 350°. Grease and flour two 9-by-5-inch loaf pans. Sift flour, baking soda, baking powder, and cinnamon.

In a large mixing bowl, combine eggs, oil, sugar, mango, raisins, nuts, and coconut; combine with dry ingredients and blend well. Pour into loaf pans and bake until breads test done, 45 to 60 minutes.

*Can substitute banana, carrot, or papaya in place of mango.